This book draws
You Tube spoke
LIFE IN 6 WORDS.
Check it out at lifein6words.com

LIFE IN 6 WORDS

COPYRIGHT © 2013 BY DARE 2 SHARE MINISTRIES, INC.

ALL RIGHTS RESERVED.

A D2S PUBLISHING BOOK

PO BOX 745323

ARVADA, CO 80006

UNLESS OTHERWISE INDICATED, ALL SCRIPTURE QUOTATIONS
ARE TAKEN FROM THE HOLY BIBLE, NEW LIVING TRANSLATION,
COPYRIGHT © 1996, 2004, 2007. USED BY PERMISSION OF
TYNDALE HOUSE PUBLISHERS, INC., CAROL STREAM, ILLINOIS
60188. ALL RIGHTS RESERVED.

SCRIPTURE QUOTATIONS MARKED NIV ARE TAKEN FROM THE
HOLY BIBLE, NEW INTERNATIONAL VERSION®, NIV®
COPYRIGHT © 1973, 1978, 1984, 2011 BY BIBLICA, INC.™
USED BY PERMISSION. ALL RIGHTS RESERVED WORLDWIDE.

AUTHOR: GREG STIER

LIFE IN 6 WORDS: THE GOSPEL SPOKEN WORD AUTHOR:
PROPAGANDA WWW.HUMBLEBEAST.COM

EDITOR: JANE DRATZ

LIFE IN 6 WORDS

ISBN: 978-0-9857352-2-7

LIBRARY OF CONGRESS CONTROL NUMBER: 2012947155

DESIGN/ILLUSTRATION BY LUKE FLOWERS CREATIVE
(LUKEFLOWERSCREATIVE.COM)

Seriously, think about it.

When you boil it all down to just a few words, what's life really about?

Acquiring the most toys?
Doing fun stuff? Helping others?
Building strong relationships?

If you ask six different people which words they'd use to describe life in just six words, you'll most likely get six different answers.

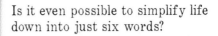

Is it even possible to simplify life down into just six words?

After all, life's complex.
It's a journey, really. So that means it's continually changing. It's fluid. And it's unique for each individual who walks their own path through it.

All that is true.

But are there some **LARGER TRUTHS** about Life that can **HELP** us make sense of this *journey* we're on? That can **HELP US** figure out what Life's about *Life* with a capital **"L"** ?

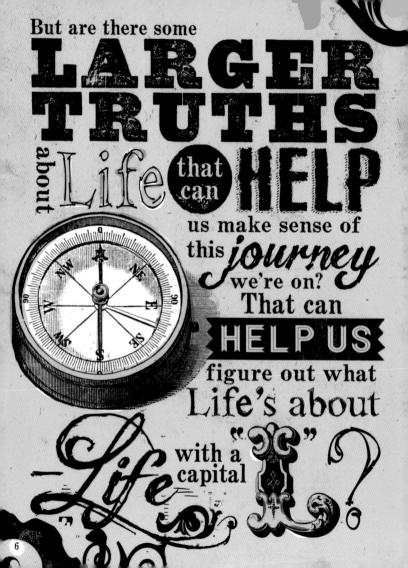

People have been asking questions about Life for thousands of years. And one of the places they've gone to for answers is the Bible.

Now most people think the Bible is a book that deserves respect. But it's a big, thick book. And many people are so intimidated by it that they've never actually read it.

So that's what this book you're holding in your hands is about. Six simple words that sum up what the Bible has to say about Life.

It's the full story of life,
The entirety of humanity
in the palm of your hand
crushed into one sentence.
GOD. OUR. SINS.
PAYING. EVERYONE.
LIFE.
The greatest story ever told,
that's hardly ever told.

You can view the video
of this spoken word poem
in its entirety at
lifein6words.com

GOD.

Yes, GOD, the maker
and giver of life,
and by life I mean
any and all matter
and substance,
seen and unseen,
what can and can't be touched.
Thoughts, images, emotions,
love, atoms and oceans.

God.

All of it His handiwork,
one of which His masterpiece
made so uniquely
that angels looked curiously.
The one thing in creation
that was made
with His imagery,
a concept so cold,
it's the reason I stay bold.
How God breathed into the man
and he became a living soul.
Formed with the intent
of being infinitely,
intimately fond,
Creator and creation
held in eternal bond.

9

GOD.

The first of our six words.
Because God's at the center of everything.

And get this. This is amazing! God not only
initiated creation, He initiated a relationship
with us, as well!

GOD CREATED US TO BE WITH HIM.

The immense, all-powerful God of the universe is also personal and relational. And He formed us humans as the "one thing in creation that was made with His imagery." He designed us uniquely "in His image" with an inner soul built for an "infinite, intimate" relationship with Him.

Maybe you're familiar with the story from the Bible about the first man and woman, Adam and Eve.

CREATING ADAM & EVE (PLEASE SEE GENESIS 2:1-25 FOR MORE DETAILED INSTRUCTIONS.)

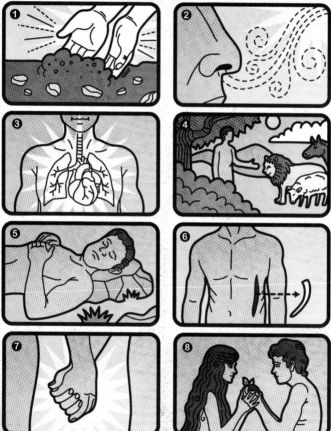

This story contains some interesting insights about God's original design for us humans. Insights that ring true deep in our souls. It describes us as—

Created in the image of God
"Then God said, 'Let us make human beings in our image, to be like us'..." (Genesis 1:26).

Created with purpose and mission
"The Lord God placed the man in the Garden of Eden to tend and watch over it" (Genesis 2:15).

Created for relationship
"When the cool evening breezes were blowing, the man and his wife heard the Lord God walking about in the garden...."
(Genesis 3:8).

Did you get that?

God created us humans in His image, with purpose and mission, to connect with Him on the deepest, most intimate level.

He created us to be in perfect relationship with Him, with each other and with His creation.

His perfect plan was that there would be no suffering, no sin, no shame - nothing to come between us and Him (or between us and others). We were made to love Him, worship Him and enjoy Him forever.

NO SUFFERING NO SIN NO SHAME

LOVE, WORSHIP & ENJOY

The deep, beautiful truth of God's relational intent for us is summarized in Psalm 100:3 with these words: "Know that the Lord is God! It is He who made us, and we are His ..." (*NIV*).

And into the deepest part of our soul, God longs to pour His love.

SIN CAME WALKING INTO THE WORLD

This truth has profound implications for us.
Physically, emotionally, spiritually and relationally.

God's original plan for us humans provided it all—
physical well-being, power and influence, emotional,
relational and spiritual fulfillment. That's why we long
for completeness in each of these dimensions of our lives.

In fact, much of the hurt and struggle we experience
in life revolves around these basic needs not being met.
Needs that God had perfectly provided for in the Garden
with Adam and Eve, but that became twisted and distorted
when sin came walking into the world through their
disobedience—and through ours.

WE LONG FOR COMPLETENESS

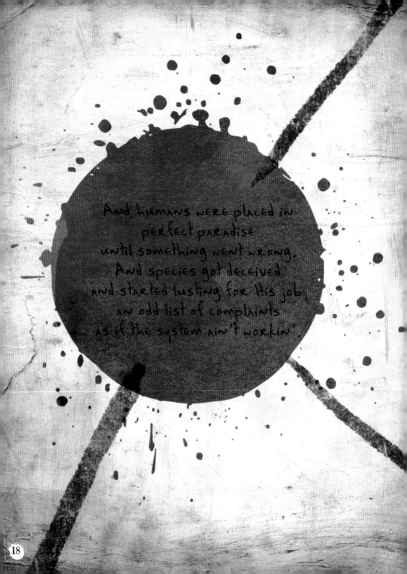

And humans were placed in
perfect paradise
until something went wrong.
And species got deceived
and started lusting for His job,
an odd list of complaints
as if the system ain't workin'.

And used that same breath
He graciously gave us
to curse Him.
And that sin seed spread
through our souls' genome,
and by the nature of your
nature, your species,
you participated in the mutiny.

OUR.

Yes, OUR sins.
It's nature inherited.
Blackened the human heart,
it was over before it started,
deceived from day one
and led away
by our own lust.
There's not a religion
in the world
that doesn't agree
that something's
wrong with us.
The question is,
what is it?
And how do we fix it?

OUR.

To put it bluntly, **OUR sins separate us from God.**

Let's be honest, sin is not a popular concept these days. No one likes to talk about it.

BUT DESPITE OUR DISCOMFORT, THERE'S REALLY NO GETTING AWAY FROM ITS UGLY REALITY.

It only takes a glance at the daily headlines to see that something has **"blackened the human heart."** Bullying, gossip, stealing, rage, rape, murder, war.

EVIL IS PRESENT IN OUR WORLD.

In its typically bold, blunt way, the Bible describes how evil got its foothold in the world.

Way back in the beginning, God invited Adam and Eve to freely love Him.

But rather than loving and trusting God and what He told them about right and wrong, they exercised their God-given freewill and disobeyed Him. They turned away from Him.

THEY CHOSE THEIR OWN PATH. THEY SINNED.

When Adam and Eve sinned, everything changed.
For all of us. The Bible puts it this way,

WHEN ADAM SINNED,
SIN ENTERED THE WORLD.
ADAM'S SIN BROUGHT DEATH,
SO DEATH SPREAD
TO EVERYONE, FOR
EVERYONE SINNED.
~ (ROMANS 5:12)

"And that seed spread through the soul's genome."

And ever since, people have been wrestling
between right and wrong – often choosing evil.
Hurting themselves and others in small and big
ways – from broken promises to mass murder.

Some people question why God gave Adam and Eve this freedom to choose between good and evil. It was an incredible, yet terrifying gift. But it was the gift that made love possible. For without the ability to freely choose, they would just be God's little robots, rather than unique individuals able to have a relationship with Him.

So sin entered our world through Adam and Eve's choice and messed it up.

But it's not just their sin that messed things up, it's **OUR** sin, too. **OUR** sin has created a separation in our relationship with a perfect and holy God.

When we take an honest look inside ourselves we see it's true. Selfishness, jealousy, cheating, lust, greed, and on and on the list goes.

We've all done wrong things. There's just no denying we're all part of the problem. We've all messed up and missed the mark. The Bible says it like this,

FOR EVERYONE HAS SINNED; WE ALL FALL SHORT OF GOD'S GLORIOUS STANDARD. – (ROMANS 3:23)

WHAT CAN BE DONE ABOUT THIS BIG PROBLEM?

GREED
PRIDE
ANGER
ENVY
REVENGE
HATE
JUDGING
CURSING

Are we eternally
separated from a God that
may or may not have existed?
But that's another subject,
let's keep grinding, besides,
trying to prove God is like
defending a lion, homie.
It don't need your help.
Just unlock the cage.
Let's move on,
on how our debt
can be paid.

Short and sweet, SIN.
the problem is SIN.
Yes, SIN. It's a cancer, an asthma,
choking out our life force,
forcing separation
from a perfect and holy God,
and the only way to get back
is to get back to perfection.
But silly us, trying to pass the course
of life without referring to a syllabus.

This is us. Heap up your good deeds,
chant, pray, meditate.
Well, all of that of course,
is spraying cologne on a corpse.
Or you could choose to ignore it,
as if something don't stink.
It's like steppin' in dog poop
and refusing to wipe your shoe.

But all of that ends with
"How good is good enough?"
Take your silly list of good deeds
and line 'em up against perfection...
Good luck.
That's life past your pay grade.
The cost of your soul,
you ain't got a big enough piggy bank...
but you could give it a shot.
But I suggest you throw away the list,
'cause even your good acts
are an extension of your selfishness.

Many people live their lives believing they can make up for the bad things they do by doing good things.

"Heap up your good deeds. Chant, pray, meditate" is their mantra. They think if they do enough good things, they'll earn their way into heaven, or nirvana or wherever.

But the Bible tells us that our holy and perfect God doesn't weigh our good and bad deeds against each other to see if we can pull out a 51 percent. God doesn't even grade on the curve. The Bible says point blank, **"nothing impure will ever enter"** heaven (Revelation 21:27, NIV). That means if you've ever sinned, just once, you're disqualified for entrance into a holy and perfect heaven.

That counts all of us out.

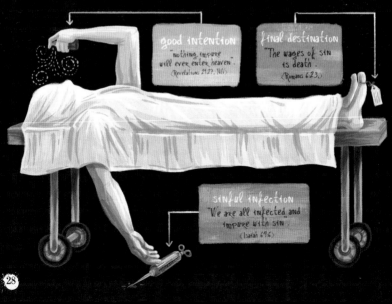

good intention
"nothing impure will ever enter heaven".
(Revelation 21:27, NIV)

final destination
"The wages of sin is death".
(Romans 6:23)

sinful infection
"We are all infected and impure with sin".
(Isaiah 64:6)

What we do qualify for is eternal separation from God in a place called hell. Romans 6:23 makes it clear that "the wages of sin is death." Bad news all around.

Through our own human efforts, we just can't be good enough to make it into a perfect heaven and stand in the presence of a perfect God. All our efforts are just "spraying cologne on a corpse."

Because SINS cannot be removed by good deeds.

Here's how the Bible puts it,
We are all infected and impure with sin.
When we display our righteous deeds,
they are nothing but filthy rags (Isaiah 64:6).

"Good enough" just doesn't cut it.

Does that mean it's all hopeless? That we're stuck in this very bad place, separated from God with no way back to Him?

But here's where it
gets interesting.
I hope you're closely listening.
Please don't get it twisted,
it's what makes our faith unique.
Here's what God says is
Part A of the gospel ...
You can't fix yourself,
quit trying, it's impossible.

Sin brings death.
Give God his breath back,
you owe Him.
Eternally separated,
and the only way to fix it
is someone dying in your place.
And that someone's
gotta be perfect
or the payment
ain't permanent.
So if and when you find
a perfect person,
get him or her to willingly
trade their perfection
for your sin and debt in.
Clearly, since the only one
that can meet God's criteria
is God, God sent Himself
as Jesus to pay the cost for us.
His righteousness, His death,
functions as

PAYMENT.

Yes, PAYMENT.

Wrote a check
with His life,
but at the resurrection
we all cheered,
'cause that means
the check cleared.

Pierced feet, pierced hands,
blood-stained Son of Man,
fullness,
forgiveness,
free passage into
the promise land.
That same breath that
God breathed into us,
God gave up to
REDEEM us.

DID YOU CATCH THAT?

OUR GOOD DEEDS

"Here's what God says is Part A of the gospel: You can't fix yourself, quit trying, it's impossible."

But while we can't fix our problem with sin ourselves, the really Good News is that God, in His great love for us, provided a way for our relationship with Him to be restored.

Not through our good deeds, but through **His** one great deed.

God's perfect, just and holy character demanded that a penalty be paid for sin. So God the Father sent His Son Jesus to earth. Fully God and fully man, Jesus lived a perfect, sinless life and died a brutal, bloody death on the cross as sacrificial payment for our sins.

IT'S THROUGH **JESUS' DEATH** AND **RESURRECTION**, THAT **THE PATH** WAS OPENED FOR OUR SINS TO **BE FORGIVEN** AND OUR RELATIONSHIP WITH GOD **RESTORED.**

Romans 3:25-26 puts it this way,

"For God presented Jesus as the sacrifice for sin. People are made right with God when they believe that Jesus sacrificed his life, shedding his blood ... God did this to demonstrate his righteousness, for he himself is fair and just, and he declares sinners to be right in his sight when they believe in Jesus."

So there you have it.
The deep, profound love of God poured out for us.

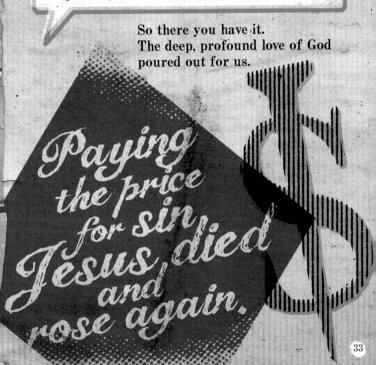

Paying the price for sin Jesus died and rose again.

Jesus paid for our sin with His life. He died in our place!

Romans 5:8 says, "But God showed his great love for us by sending Christ to die for us while we were still sinners." As He died, He cried out the words

"it is finished"

declaring that the price
for our sins was paid
completely. He died
the death that we deserved
so that we could truly live!

And with His resurrection from the dead three days later, He proved that He was who He claimed to be, God in the flesh. Jesus "wrote a check with His life, and at the resurrection we all cheered, 'cause that means the check cleared!"

WHILE WE WERE STILL SINNERS

And anyone and everyone,
and by EVERYONE,
I mean EVERYONE,
who puts their faith and trust
in Him and Him alone
can stand in full confidence of
God's forgiveness.

EVERYONE.

Jesus extends the **FREE** gift of salvation and a restored relationship with God to everyone!

And that means EVERYONE— from the most devout saint to the most notorious sinner.

EVERYONE
who trusts in Him **alone** has eternal **life.**

Back in Jesus' day, many of the "religious" people lost sight of the truth that God yearns for a relationship with us. Instead, they thought relating to God was just about a bunch of religious do's and don'ts where people try to earn their way back to God by keeping the rules.

"RELIGIOUS" DO'S & DON'TS

YOU ARE HERE ↓

So Jesus' invitation to eternal life through believing in Him was radical, revolutionary and distinctly uncomfortable for the "religious" of His day.

And it still is.

Because Jesus' salvation message of love and grace embraces gossips and bullies. Losers and liars. Cutters and porn addicts. It's freely available to anyone and **EVERYONE.**

Including **you.**

All it takes to enter into this amazing, life-changing, personal relationship with God is faith in Jesus alone to forgive your sins and give you eternal life.

Once you put your trust in Him alone, God welcomes you with open arms.

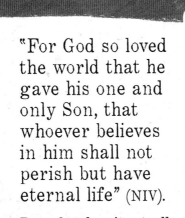

JOHN 3:16

says it this way,

"For God so loved the world that he gave his one and only Son, that whoever believes in him shall not perish but have eternal life" (NIV).

But what does it actually mean to "believe in Him"?

WHEN THE BIBLE USES THE WORD "*Believe*" HERE, IT MEANS "TO TRUST IN AND RELY UPON COMPLETELY."

So believing in Jesus takes more than just "knowing" in your head that Jesus is God, for the Bible tells us that even the spiritual forces of darkness know this truth and tremble.

TRULY "BELIEVING" MEANS TRUSTING IN AND *fully* RELYING ON JESUS ALONE TO *forgive you* FOR ALL YOUR SINS.

Because a restored relationship with God for all eternity is not achieved by good deeds, but received as a gift through faith.

IT'S **NOT** A MATTER OF **TRYING**, BUT TRUSTING, IN JESUS ALONE.

And here's
what the promise is,
that you are guaranteed
full access
to return to perfect unity.
By simply believing in Christ
and Christ alone,
you are receiving
LIFE.
Yes, LIFE.

LIFE

LIFE.

The impact on your life when you trust in Jesus is astounding!

Jesus floods your soul with the joy and peace that come from being forgiven for your past and set free for a future with Him. Through faith in Jesus, you are saved from hell and assured of heaven.

John 10:28 says it like this, "I give them eternal life, and they will never perish. No one can snatch them away from me."

The hope of heaven is a fabulous thing!

But there's more. This abundant, eternal life available through Jesus doesn't just start after you die and go to heaven.

NO, LIFE with Jesus starts now and lasts forever.

Because as a believer in Jesus, you are "guaranteed full access to return to perfect unity" NOW.

NOW

AND

forever

FULL ACCESS

GUARANTEED!

Just THINK of it!

You can talk to the God of the universe any time of the day or night, no matter where you are or who you are with, no matter what hurt or joy is unfolding in your life, no matter how far you might fall or what heights you might soar to.

And God connects with you, as well, through the love letter of His Bible, helping you discover how to follow Him on this new, exciting adventure. Plus, from the moment you believe in Jesus, His Holy Spirit comes to live inside you and guide you.

It's wild, actually!
God and you reconnected back into an "infinite, intimate" relationship, now and forever.

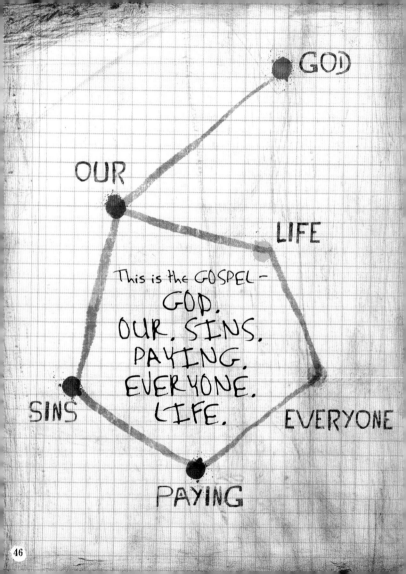

GOD

OUR

LIFE

This is the GOSPEL —
GOD.
OUR. SINS.
PAYING.
EVERYONE.
LIFE.

SINS

EVERYONE

PAYING

LIFE in 6 words.
The GOSPEL.

But you can't just **read about it.**
You have to **believe it** –
believe it is truth and life.
You have to **take hold of it.**
Embrace it. Trust it.

Are you ready
to accept the gift of life that
Jesus extends to everyone
who puts their trust in Him?

Is there anything holding you back?

You can start a new relationship with God **RIGHT NOW!**

Your heart and soul can be transformed by putting your trust in Jesus alone. Will you put your trust in Him? If you're ready to make this life-changing decision, do it now.

Then let God know that you've put your faith in Jesus through a prayer. It's not that the prayer itself saves you – it's only what God does in your soul when you trust in Christ alone that does that!

So you might say something like this -

"Dear God,
I know that my sins have broken my relationship with you and that nothing I could do could ever change that. But right now, I believe that Jesus died in my place and rose again from the dead. I trust in Him to forgive me for my sins. Through faith in Him, I am entering an eternal relationship with you. Thank you for this free gift!

Amen."

1

If you've just put **your trust in Jesus,** be sure to connect with the person who gave you this book or with someone you know who is already a Jesus follower.

2

They will help you get **plugged into a church** where you can grow in your relationship with God alongside others.

TAKE NEW LIFE CARD

GO AHEAD 3 SPACES

START

SHARE A
LIFE CARD

3

FREE

For help getting started on your new adventure with God, go to **lifein6words.com** for a free downloadable copy of Now Grow. In the "Connect with God" section, just indicate that you've made a decision to trust Jesus. You'll find the **free download** there.

EXTRA
TURN. GO
AGAIN!

MAKE A
LIFE MOVE.

steps

And now tell **someone else** about Jesus. This is news that's too good to keep to yourself!

GOOD
NEWS!

4

DRAW A
LIFE CARD!

51

Or maybe you aren't ready to make a decision and still have more questions about God. That's understandable, too.

Figuring out what you believe about Jesus is **a big decision.**

2

If you want to explore the GOSPEL further, check out **lifein6words.com.** You'll find a video of the *Life in 6 Words* spoken word poetry found in this book, along with other helpful information about Jesus.

3

Check out the video, talk to your friend who gave you this book, **ask questions, think about it and then decide.**

Life

big question

START

EXTRA TURN, GO AGAIN!